D1000264

WITHDRAWN

Minor League

Minor League

Photographs by Andrea Modica

Smithsonian Institution Press, Washington and London
Published in association with Constance Sullivan Editions

This series was developed and produced for the Smithsonian Institution Press by
Constance Sullivan Editions

Series editor:
Constance Sullivan

Smithsonian editor:
Amy Pastan

Designed by Katy Homans

The paper used in this publication meets the minimum requirements of the
American National Standard for Permanence of Paper for Printed Library Materials
Z39.48-1984.

First edition

Printed by Meridian Printing, East Greenwich, RI, USA
Duotone separations by Thomas Palmer

cover: Billy Coleman, Scott Gully, and Bert Inman, pitchers, Oneonta Yankees, Oneonta, New York, 1991

The photographs were made in part with the support of the New York State Council on the Arts.

Photographs courtesy Julie Saul Gallery, New York City.

The photographer wishes to thank Sam and John Nader, Jack Gillis, Mark Rose, and
the New York Yankees Organization for making these photographs possible.

When did you become interested in making photographs?

In college I studied painting and printmaking, then I began welding metal and making sculpture, and finally, in my senior year, I became interested in photography. I went to SUNY Purchase where there was a lot of photographic equipment available to students, including two 8x10 cameras. I started almost immediately using the big camera because I liked the physicality of moving it around and feeling like I was actually making something. The slower photographic process of carrying around the camera, setting it up, composing the picture, and processing the film appealed to me. I guess it just suits my metabolism.

Were you concerned that such a cumbersome camera might limit what you could do?

No. As I said, prior to studying photography I was welding metal for sculpture, so I got used to working with large equipment and heavy material.

Does working with an 8x10 view camera affect your rapport with the person you are photographing, inasmuch as their awareness of you is different than if you were using a small camera?

This issue is extremely important in my work, especially the portraiture. I have never used a small camera and it's difficult for me to imagine running around shooting inconspicuously and not having a rapport with the person I'm photographing. When I photograph someone, they respond to me as much as I respond to them, and their response to who I am, as well as to the camera and setting, becomes a part of the picture. Also, the amount of time that elapses between when I ask a person to pose for a picture and when I snap the shutter has an effect on their portrait.

How did you come to photograph Barbara, the little girl who often appears in your Treadwell, New York, series?

I began photographing her in 1986 when I was working with an anthropologist on a project about women farmers. While driving around upstate New York, where I live and teach, we saw a family sprawled out on their lawn and front porch. We stopped to ask if I could photograph them and discovered that there were fourteen children in the family, some of whom were married and living in the house with their spouses and children along with various boyfriends and girlfriends. I think there were about twenty-one people living under one roof at that time. That first day, I took the picture of two children clasped in their mother's arms that has since been published and exhibited a lot. I brought back photographs to show them, which they loved, so I keep bringing them photographs.

Does your relationship with this family, which has evolved over time, influence the way they look in your pictures?

Of course. This is a very large family, many of them did not make it through grammar school, they are on and off of welfare, and involved with some violence. Their values are very different from mine, but through this project over the years we've found some common ground, in addition to which my fears and prejudices have been challenged. For me that is largely what the photographic process is about.

Describe how you actually get someone to sit for a portrait.

Well, I say, "Would you mind if I take your photograph?" Then I explain, before the 8x10 view camera comes out of the car, that because of the slow process they'll have to stay still for several minutes. I tell them who I am and what I'm doing and try to get them just to sit in front of the camera and see what happens—whether they get close together or far apart. And, at that point, I usually let them know that I'll give them a photograph. So that's how it starts. But the beauty of an ongoing project is that after the first explanation, no further explanations are necessary, which is one of the reasons why I like to photograph groups, such as a family or a baseball team.

Do you preconceive your pictures or direct your subject?

I have a very good sense of how far away from things I should stand to get what I want into the frame, but I still need to decide what to include in the picture. Sometimes I might respond to a piece of light coming into the room, or to something hanging on the wall, and I'll ask somebody to sit near that object. What's very interesting to me, of course, is just how the person sits near that thing, their relationship to whatever it is (which could be another person). For example, in that first picture we talked about, of the two children with their mother, because the kids were so young and the exposure was rather long (maybe a fifth of a second), the mother was literally holding them still. Her caress seems at once loving and restraining. But then that hand entered the picture frame.

Do you think of these as documentary photographs?

Absolutely not. I really think about them as fantasies, fables or fairy tales.

Are you a portrait photographer?

My photographs are consistently of people.

Your work is usually about closed societies, little worlds unto themselves, each with its own set of rules. Why does that appeal to you?

I usually photograph a group or even a person because there's something about them that I don't understand, or am afraid of, or maybe have some prejudice against.

How did your series of pictures of baseball players come about?

I was on a date and we went to a baseball game. Now I had absolutely no interest in or knowledge of the game at that point, but I live in a tiny town and one thing you can do in the summer is go to a ball game. Although I wasn't interested in the game, I could get a close look at these players, because in minor league baseball you can sit right near the field. They're very close. So this pitcher walked in front of me and I noticed his cheekbones. I thought, "My, what fabulous cheekbones, and how that little cap sets them off." While I watched the game, I wondered who on earth would choose this for a career. I mean, hitting this little ball around seemed so silly in a way. These guys work very hard, they make very little money, and maybe two percent of minor league players go on to the major leagues. Knowing that, I was really curious about why they would do it, and I thought about this so much that it occurred to me, almost in a dream, to photograph these players. And I'll tell you something, I woke up in a cold sweat. I was so scared of this particular project.

Why did you make portraits of the players rather than pictures of the game being played?

Because of my intense curiosity about them. After putting it off for a while, I contacted the team owner and asked if I could do this. He said yes if I also got the team manager to agree. Sometimes when I was working with these guys they exhibited certain behavior that made me very uncomfortable, which was hard to deal with. But a certain discomfort was also a part of the family project.

You find this tension surrounding your differences with certain people stimulating?

I figure that if photographing a situation makes me *this* nervous there must be something for me to learn, and that makes it worth doing. It's not only about taking good pictures.

**But formal issues are obviously important. Your
pictures are so beautifully resolved, even when
they deal with disturbing subject matter.**

I think the subject matter is what determines the formal arrangement of
the photograph. For instance, one of the baseball players had his nickname,
"Willy," written on his shirt, and that's what attracted me in terms of
wanting to photograph him. So I got in very, very close. I start off wanting
to photograph something in the world and as long as I go with that the
formal elements fall into place.

**Many of your baseball portraits show a
camaraderie or closeness between two or more
players. Are you consciously exploring their
emotional and psychological relationships?**

In any situation, once I set up the camera unexpected things start to unfold.
Initially, I might be interested in someone's cheekbones, but when I'm ready
to take the guy's picture maybe his buddy comes along. What happens
between the buddies? In the pictures of couples or groups, what becomes
apparent is perhaps a power play. Sometimes it appears that one person
has a little more power over the other. Remember, these players are highly
competitive but they also really need each other—they need to work
together closely. Well, one day two players showed up for a photograph—
now, I hadn't asked them to pose together—but the pitching coach later
explained to me that one was a shortstop and the other a second baseman,
and they were "married" on the field. It was curious that they wanted to be
photographed together. And when you put two people wearing the same
uniform together in a picture, you suddenly notice their differences. One of
these guys looks much older, more mature and maybe a little bit tougher,
and they like looking tough for the camera. Right? Their bats are going in
opposite directions—this is all their own doing—and then you move down
to their feet and their toes are touching. It astonishes me that somehow the
notion about their being "married" on the field came out in the photograph.

Will you continue working on the baseball series?

The newer pictures in the series are opening up formally and I feel that there is much more I can do in that direction. Also, having photographed for two seasons, I rephotographed last year's Oneonta Yankees in Greensboro, so I followed them up the ranks and I would like to follow these guys up one more level.

Your portraits have a formal, almost classical look.

I think the baseball pictures look more formal because there is so little time to shoot them. Some of these pictures were taken in a minute or two, and most were done in the shade or on overcast days, which gives the effect of an outdoor studio, where all of the pores and pimples and scars are very clearly defined. That, combined with the platinum print, or contact print, makes the photographs very descriptive.

And you like that specificity of description.

That's part of what photography's always been about for me. It's one of the reasons I started working with the big camera and making platinum prints.

Why are you so taken with the platinum-palladium printing process?

I enjoy it technically, which probably comes from having studied so many different mediums and always having been interested in making things. The platinum print is just one more thing to make. It also gives a more extended scale, so there's that much more description. Also, I like having the prints *in* the paper instead of sitting on top of the paper. I enjoy the way a print feels in my hand.

What have your influences been?

I'm very interested in Italian painting and Italian reliquary art—taking a tiny piece of a leg bone and making a big golden leg. I like the idea of making much ado about nothing, maybe that's why reliquaries are so interesting to me.

Mike Draper, pitcher, New York Yankees, Fort Lauderdale, Florida, 1992

Jorge Posada, catcher, Oneonta Yankees, Oneonta, New York, 1991

Oneonta, New York, 1992

Mark Hubbard, outfielder, Greensboro Hornets, Greensboro, North Carolina, 1992

Billy Coleman, Scott Gully, and Bert Inman, pitchers, Oneonta Yankees, Oneonta, New York, 1991

Ray Suplee and Kraig Hawkins, outfielders, Oneonta Yankees, Oneonta, New York, 1992

Kraig Hawkins, outfielder, and Richard Turentine, pitcher, Oneonta Yankees, Oneonta, New York, 1992

Alvaro Espinoza, infielder, and Hensley Meulens, outfielder, New York Yankees, Fort Lauderdale, Florida, 1992

Nick Del Vecchio, infielder, Oneonta Yankees, Oneonta, New York, 1992

R. D. Long, infielder, Oneonta Yankees, Oneonta, New York, 1992

Ray Suplee and Kraig Hawkins, outfielders, Oneonta Yankees, Oneonta, New York, 1992

Mike Buddie, pitcher, and Robert Hinds, outfielder, Oneonta Yankees, Oneonta, New York, 1992

Jorge Posada, catcher, Oneonta Yankees, Oneonta, New York, 1991

Matt Luke, outfielder, Oneonta Yankees, Oneonta, New York, 1992

Eric Knowles, infielder, Oneonta Yankees, Oneonta, New York, 1992

Andy Croghan, pitcher, and Tom Wilson, catcher, Oneonta Yankees, Oneonta, New York, 1991

Jeff Johnson, pitcher, New York Yankees, Fort Lauderdale, Florida, 1992

Steve Phillips, outfielder, Oneonta Yankees, Oneonta, New York, 1991

José Piñeda, catcher, Greensboro Hornets, Greensboro, North Carolina, 1992

Sandi Santiago and Mike Buddie, pitchers, Oneonta Yankees, Oneonta, New York, 1992

Andy Croghan, pitcher, Oneonta Yankees, Oneonta, New York, 1991

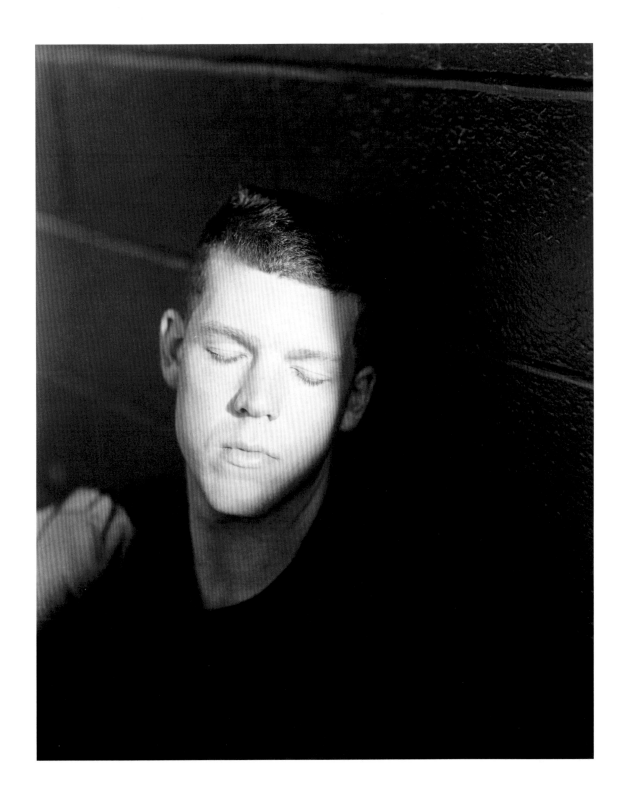

Kent Wallace, pitcher, Oneonta Yankees, Oneonta, New York, 1992

Tom Wilson, catcher, Greensboro Hornets, Greensboro, North Carolina, 1992

Roger Burnett and Steve Anderson, infielders, Oneonta Yankees, Oneonta, New York, 1991

Oneonta, New York, 1992

Andrea Modica

Andrea Modica's work is in such major collections as the Metropolitan Museum of Art and the Museum of Modern Art in New York City, the National Museum of American Art, Smithsonian Institution, the San Francisco Museum of Modern Art, and the Bibliothèque Nationale in Paris; and she was included in *Women Photographers* (Harry N. Abrams, 1990), sandwiched significantly between soul sisters Sally Mann and Judith Joy Ross. Modica remains, however, a photographer's photographer. Like so many emerging young artists, much of her rather extraordinary output has yet to be discovered by a broader public. This group of baseball pictures is her first published portfolio.

Modica was born in Brooklyn in 1960 and grew up there. Inspired by a dynamic high school art teacher, she began taking summer courses at the Brooklyn Museum and traveling to Manhattan to visit galleries and buy art supplies on Canal Street. She attended the State University of New York's campus at Purchase, a college devoted to art studies, where she painted and sculpted ("I thought I had found God when I welded metal," she says) until photography eclipsed nearly everything else. Early on, with the encouragement of teacher Jed Devine, she started making palladium and platinum prints, and she uses a combination of these processes almost exclusively to this day. Combined with her use of a traditional 8x10 view camera, the platinum–palladium method gives Modica's intensely of-the-moment work a warm, rich, almost classical feel.

Photography became, Modica says, "This thing that I lived for." Her early subjects were the women in her family, her friends and neighbors, but it wasn't until she began to make pictures in the New Haven psychiatric halfway house where she worked full time that Modica hit on the sort of project and approach that would define her work. She started the job in her first year out of college and continued to work there nights during her two years at Yale graduate school. Sleeping overnight at the halfway house, where she was available for crisis intervention, Modica would often get up in the morning and take pictures of the residents. "The first year was a little scary," she says, "but by the second year I realized that there was very little difference, if any, between (us) and (them). And I didn't want to take pictures of them because they were different from me. I wanted to photograph what was the same."

This unforced, unaffected empathy characterized all of Modica's photographs. During the period when she was making her halfway house portraits, in the mid-1980s, she was also commuting regularly from Yale to New York, where she was busy photographing the students at her old Catholic girls' high school, Brooklyn's Fontbonne Hall, searching for roots and reflections. A Fulbright grant took her to Sicily for six months in 1990, digging even deeper into the past. The project, planned as a portrait of Sicilian women, broadened to involve, as all of Modica's work does, "photographing things that I may not understand and trying to find what I have in common with other people."

Perhaps the best expression of that approach is in an ongoing series of photographs Modica began shortly after graduating from Yale in 1985 and moving to Oneonta, New York, to teach photography and drawing at the state university there. Driving around "looking for people," she found a plump little girl named Barbara and her family of fourteen, many of whom were hanging out on the front porch of their rundown house. Modica's first picture—Barbara and another child looking lost and fragile in a parental embrace—is one of her most engaging. With that photograph, a bond with Barbara and her extended clan was formed that endured and resulted in some of the decade's most compassionate and unnerving pictures of the American family.

Pictures of Barbara and her family were included in Modica's first gallery show, a group exhibit at New York's Lieberman & Saul in 1988 that placed her platinum–palladium prints alongside those of Jan Groover and Madoka Takaji. Her first solo show there, in 1991, included early work from the series of baseball portraits she's been making over the past two years. Curious about the "big, brawling macho guys" in the local farm team, the Oneonta Yankees, Modica began a delicate, probing investigation of masculinity and camaraderie that, like all her work, balances attraction and reserve, sympathy and insight. Modica, shrugging off a fancier interpretation, is smartly matter of fact about her baseball pictures. "Like the girls' school, like the halfway house, like the town in Sicily, like Barbara and her family, it's a group of people that let me come back and photograph again and again," she says. "Which is what I do."

— Vincent Aletti

Technical Information

From early on, Andrea Modica has used an 8x10 field camera. Her current model is a wooden one made by Phillips & Sons, which she bought in 1988 in anticipation of her trip to Sicily. She's used the same camera, the same lens (a Dagor 10¾), and the same tripod ever since. She credits the training she received at Yale under such teachers as Richard Benson and Tod Papageorge with preparing her for the rigors of the 8x10. While there, she says, "I photographed more than I thought was physically possible. They had me working with an 8x10 like I was using a 35mm." The ease she developed then allows Modica to achieve a look that's both unusually spontaneous and carefully composed.

She photographs in natural light or, occasionally, with the available illumination of a nearby light bulb. Flashes and strobes are not part of her equipment: "If I can't see the light, I don't use it."

Modica has always printed her own work, always with a mixture of platinum and palladium processes. She varies the tonal range to suit the subject at hand, making the baseball work cooler than the warm-toned series with Barbara and her family. Why platinum? "It's full in terms of tonal range, complete, and beautiful. I'm a sucker for beauty."